NO MORE STORIES ABOUT THE MOON

J. Bradley

© 2016 Lucky Bastard Press, Oakland, CA

ISBN 978-0-9964099-5-7

All rights reserved. This book may not be reproduced, in whole or in part including illustrations, in any form (beyond that copying permitted by 107 and 108 of the U.S Copyright Law and except by reviewers for the public press), without written permission from the author(s).

Cover illustration © 2016 Molly Mule.

CONTENTS

On Writing "How An Autobot Sunk The Titanic"	1
Carotid	5
Date Night	6
Thread Counting	9
Raymond Carver's Dance Party	10
In The Company Of Leaves	13
Waffles and Honey	14
No More Stories About The Moon	15
Sauvignon Fierce	17
Acknowledgements	21
About the Author	22

ON WRITING "HOW AN AUTOBOT SUNK THE TITANIC"

I started with the idea of a time-travelling Autobot, but not as a time traveling vehicle, like a DeLorian or the Jet Car from *The Adventures of Buckaroo Banzai*. I needed a vehicle that looked domesticated, yet unafraid to toss a catch phrase like "prepared to get grilled" before hitting evil in the face with its grill while in vehicle form and I found this vehicle in the Dodge Caravan that "accidentally" hit Stephen King. I drew the Caravan on a sheet of paper and using my pencil like the blade of a monarch, I knighted the drawing *Domesticus*, the Autobot programmed to teach other Autobots home economics. This obviously made Domesticus a very, very sad Autobot, as robots have no need for home economics, giving me an easy motive for my metallic protagonist.

I began the story in the middle, where Domesticus—in his Dodge Caravan form—raced toward Stephen King, trying to stop him before he thought of

Dreamcatcher (the cause of the second Autobot holocaust in the year 4137). As Domesticus roars toward the catalyst of his grandfather's destruction, his human captor, Brian Smith, accesses Domesticus's memory banks and we see how we've reached this point: the poor attendance of Domesticus's home economic courses, his voracious appetite for reading that lead to his discovery of *Dreamcatcher* and the devious binary code within the word "shit-weasels" that annihilated almost all of the Autobots, his plans to steal energon from Megatron and use it to fuel the time machine in the Ark to travel back to Lovell, Maine on June 19, 1999 at 4:20 p.m. to confront Stephen King and save his fellow Autobots from this horrible disaster. Then, back in the present, Brian has this moment where he, too, can do something important as a man who is regarded as insignificant in his own life (I was almost tempted to make Brian a home economics teacher for a school of people who have no sense of taste or touch but that would have been a bit heavy-handed). That's what gave Brian the strength to override Domesticus's controls, aiming him *at* King instead of *toward* King. It's even more poetic when Brian yells, "Prepare to get grilled!" before hitting the accelerator—the very catch phrase Domesticus had planned to use in battle, but never got to. Because of

Brian's monkeying around with Domesticus's circuitry, and the impact of the accident, Domesticus's spark gets jarred out of his body and sucked into time. Then we get a flash-forward of Stephen King sitting behind a table at a Barnes & Noble in New York with stacks of *Dreamcatcher* surrounding him, people lined up, waiting to get a signature. I used dialogue to show the audience how if it hadn't been for the accident, King never would have written *Dreamcatcher*, illustrating one of those spiffy time-travel paradoxes we writers use to teach important lessons about how you can't change the past, only the future.

But that wasn't enough. I had to make sure that I drove the message home. So we go back to the *Titanic* veering toward the iceberg. Domesticus's spark, now inhabiting the *Titanic*, decided to defeat the iceberg, the representation of all of his fears and doubts. Domesticus finally gets to yell, "Prepare to get grilled!" before realizing that the iceberg is impossible to best. So then he whispers, "Just kidding" before turning away. The iceberg still gashes the hull. Many people still die. Domesticus's spark fades away into nothing.

To make sure the ending isn't quite as sad, though, I added that Celine Dion, aged eight, ends up trapped on the *Titanic* as it sinks. I used that classic flashback technique to show Domesticus using his last bit spark to send a message to his present self, ensuring that he kidnaps Celine Dion in his travels and leaves her in the *Titanic* before going to see Stephen King. The last image we see is the angel wings in Dion's cheeks clipped by arctic water.

CAROTID

I take a packet of steak sauce out of my left breast pocket. I ignore the dotted-line instructions for where to tear, swallowing the plastic corner so it doesn't get stuck between my teeth. The tang slaps me awake enough for my hands to return like planchettes to the keyboard. I wait until my coworker in the next cube has her back turned toward me, then pull the chewed packet out of my mouth. I've got three packets left and it's 2:12 p.m. on a Monday. If only the cafeteria didn't close early today.

DATE NIGHT

"Why did you knock on the door instead of bursting through the wall of my apartment?"

"I only do that to houses, and only when making commercials. The ad men said that invading apartments is too depressing. People who live in apartments normally can only afford Flavor Aid—so the folks in marketing tell me."

I remembered the way the djinni that came from Pavement's vinyl album cover sleeve of *Wowie Zowie* had looked at me when I wished to take the Kool-Aid Man out on a date.

"Are you sure you want this? You can have anything you want, money, cars, superpowers, anything."

I nodded.

At the tapas restaurant, the Kool-Aid Man and I share stuffed grape leaves, a cheese plate, bell peppers stuffed with Gorgonzola and sweetened chorizo. I try not to watch the digested food disappear into his artificial-cherry-colored plasma.

"That was delicious," he rasps. "Can we step away for a moment? I need a cigarette."

Outside, we lean against the restaurant. He digs a pack of Lucky Strikes and a black Bic out of his blue swim trunks. He pulls a cigarette out of the pack using only his mouth, then lights it.

"I'm not allowed to drink booze or pop pills. It's in my contract. Smoking helps calm my nerves after spending hours and hours with child actors, bitter adults working for scale. I'm having a good time, by the way. I forgot what it was like to have dinner with a decent person."

"I figured you needed a nice night out." I say. "I've always wanted to meet you, find out what you would be like away from the cameras, the children, the animation. I'm having a good time, too."

"Anything else you'd want to find out?" His right eyebrow forms a come-hither arch.

Fifteen minutes later, we're back at my place. He tries pinning me against the wall to kiss me; I feel like an insect on his windshield. We try fooling around on the couch, his glass mouth lukewarm against my neck. I don't reach into his shorts. I already know what he doesn't have.

"Kool-Aid, sweetheart, this isn't working. Our bodies are just too different. I hope you aren't disappointed."

"You're just like the others." He picks his yellow Hawaiian shirt off the floor, puts it on, and walks out the door. Even in his anger and frustration, he still used the door instead of bursting through a wall. I might call him tomorrow and see if we can go out again.

THREAD COUNTING

I smother Daniel's face into the pillow, then pivot his head slightly to the left. The blinds hold back the sunlight like a crowd, the straggler showing me the faded tattoo of a drooling pelican on Daniel's left shoulder. I quit him as I prepare him.

There are fresh batteries in the clock above the dresser, a back-up condom in case the first one doesn't stay on or won't go on. Daniel keeps his head cocked to the left, staring at the open closet, t-shirts gathering his skin to add to the collection.

There will be an ending here, clothing gathered, small talk forced; I'll never ask him about the pelican.

RAYMOND CARVER'S DANCE PARTY

"Fill me with your seed," Hillary yelled into my ear between pitter-pattering beats, a metallic voice singing something about the beat dropping and the party never stopping. The thin, plastic cup of Malibu, pineapple, cranberry, and ice almost fell out of my hands.

"Where? When?"

"Ten minutes. The handicapped bathroom. Make sure the door guy isn't looking when you go in." Hillary danced her way through the floor toward the front of the club. I finished the pureed island, looked into the cup.

"What should I do?" I asked the ice. The sweat of the cup nipped at my fingertips. "What should I do?" I poured one of the cubes into my mouth, snapped it with my teeth; the ghost of 1992 melted into my tongue.

No glove, no love. The brain freeze sounded like a mix of Ervin "Magic" Johnson, Madonna, and Rosie Perez.

"What if it's just her mouth?" The second cube cracked in my mouth. This time the ghost of 1992 crocheted the lyrics to "Another One Bites The Dust" onto my gums. Even if the past was down with such a hot mistake, I knew Hillary wasn't into appetizers.

If this were a romance novel, the song that played during our first kiss while we looked into each other's eyes in the handicapped bathroom would be a power ballad. We would use verbs like *ravage, thrust, pull*, adjectives like *aching, flushed, engorged, heated*. If this were a literary novel, there would be an internal conflict where I would decide what my love/lust for Hillary was worth by playing "Who's The Father," seeing as how Hillary would never love me back, no matter how many orgasms I gave her, how many promises I made her. If this were an after-school special, she would get pregnant and we both might survive an STI scare—depending on the mood of the writer while writing it. If this were a John Hughes film, we would end up together in the bathroom, but not end up getting it on because a) someone would walk in while we were in a compromising position and the audience would laugh at us because being walked in on while your pants are down is funny to everyone but you or b) we would have a heart-to-heart about why we shouldn't do this because we're in love with other people and it would be believable and something from Crowded House would play us out of the bathroom.

When I bit into the third cube, the ghost of 1992 opened a *Choose Your Own Adventure* book entitled *A Night At The Club*. Hillary and I were on the cover in our club clothes. Page 102 confirmed that she'd said, "Give me your seed"

On the bottom of the page it read: "If you want Craig to follow Hillary into the bathroom, turn to page 73" and "If you want Craig to stay at the bar, turn to page 67."

The fourth ice cube said nothing.

This is not how I helped make you, Bobby. One day, I'll tell you how you were made. One day.

iN THE COMPANY OF LEAVES

It gave up its skin without a fight. No threats to tell its father. No summoning reinforcements. I slipped on the tree trunk, snapped the gauntlets around my wrists, my fingers sliding gently into its hands.

"What the hell are you wearing?"

Mitch, his pack of hairless wolves, stomp over, their wide strides closing the distance between us quickly. I press a button on my gauntlet. Panels all over my torso slide down, leaves floating out of them gently, then swarming over my body.

"Wanna find out?"

Mitch's hands respond. A leaf slices open his left wrist. Another takes two fingers. He rolls on the ground, hemorrhaging in blood and tears. Mitch's pack turns, walks away quietly.

I tuck the notebook beneath my arm, look both ways before walking down the steps of my house. One of these days, what they ruin will wrap around me like lacerating armor.

WAFFLES AND HONEY

I walk in the bicycle lane with your voice. Traffic in my left ear chops and screws part of your sentences. I don't care if I can't understand part of what you say; you are a taut ribbon.

I'm working for the day I lumber through the door, and you are sitting on the couch, eraser in your mouth, and you cock your head toward me and ask how my day was, where I don't have to walk with traffic just to have an excuse to hear you.

NO MORE STORIES ABOUT THE MOON

"Do you think Jesus believes in giving women oral?" Nancy stares at the cancer spreading slowly across the moon.

"I think that's still considered sodomy, even if Jesus did it."

"That's probably why we don't really believe in Jesus. I mean, he could work miracles, but couldn't let Mary Magdalene ride his face once in awhile?"

"He'd rather eat ham than pussy."

Nancy and I watch the cancer spread further.

"When we have a child, I hope it's a boy, and I hope he's old enough so I can show him a lunar eclipse and explain that's God's way of showing men how their mouth should act when a woman willingly opens their galaxy to him: prayerful, slowly widening."

"What if he wants to eat ham instead?"

"His cheeks will burn like Sodom and Gomorrah by my hand. Or because his mother is talking about giving women oral."

"So while you give life, you can take its dignity away?"

Nancy nods. Our lawn chairs creak as we settle in, her thumb rubbing a halo into my palm.

SAUVIGNON FIERCE

I add the plastic bag carrying a half-clean lunch container to the growing cityscape on the dining room table. I use a broken UHF antenna to practice showing the others how to make it through alleyways of dusty dinner plates, the carefulness of looking around the corners of the shot-out tenements of wine glasses stained with week-old Barefoot merlot. Only then, I would say, only then would they capture this last parcel.

* * *

My father thought furniture was the solution. A new living room table to keep the rug from escaping. A bed with no memory. Drawings of places worth traveling to, worth staring at. Two TVs doubling as murder weapons (from the right height). A DVD player with no remote. "Make the effort," he said.

* * *

Today's mail falls onto torn envelopes, the accordions-in-progress of bank statements, Express ads quietly shaming me into an eating disorder and a straight shave. My cat rubs herself against my legs, chases after a bug, a ghost. She climbs to the top of the refrigerator, talks to the cat upstairs.

***

Natalie didn't say anything as she followed me across the trail of dirty laundry, spent candy wrappers, flecks of faded receipts leading into my bedroom. Black curtains hid the detergent stains on the carpet. My father said that they'd keep the sunlight out when he put them up. I used them to hide the gap-toothed grimaces of the blinds.

***

Every June 15, I go over to my father's place, drink boilermakers. We drag out a mattress he bought from Goodwill, pour the remainder of the plastic-bottle whiskey onto it, tuck a book of matches in. I always offer to bring whiskey that comes in a glass bottle, but he says plastic is the only way the next morning can feel like my mother.

***

The UHF antenna wobbles as I trace my route, rolling out from the corner of the empty Amazon box, past the dirty-wine-glass sentries, into the tower of dusty plates. I imagine a page pointing behind him, the door ajar. He'll warn me that I'll only find bandages if I keep looking.

***

Leigh didn't care about the Petri dish of my living room. Tom didn't care that the last time my sheets touched water was three months ago on Valentine's Day. Gina didn't care about the evolving ruins of my kitchen, clearing out thickets of pots and pans from the sink. My father keeps telling me "Make the effort." I'm waiting for someone other than him to tell me the same.

ACKNOWLEDGEMENTS

The author would like to acknowledge the following magazines in which some of these stories first appeared:

"Carotid" was first published in *Six Sentences*

"Thread Counting" was first published in *Matchbook Literary Magazine*

"Raymond Carver's Dance Party" was first published in *kill author*

"Waffles and Honey" was first published in *Stripped: A Collection of Anonymous Flash Fiction*

"Sauvignon Fierce" was first published in *WhiskeyPaper*

ABOUT THE AUTHOR

J. Bradley is the author of the graphic poetry collection *The Bones of Us* (YesYes Books, 2014) with art by Adam Scott Mazer, the linked story collection *The Adventures of Jesus Christ, Boy Detective* (Pelekinesis) and *Pick How You Will Revise A Memory* (Robocup Press, 2016), a collection of prose poems disguised as Yelp reviews. His flash fiction chapbook *Neil* won *Five [Quarterly]*'s 2015 e-chapbook contest for fiction. He runs the Central Florida reading series/micro chapbook publisher There Will Be Words and lives at iheartfailure.net.

www.ingramcontent.com/pod-product-compliance
Lightning Source LLC
Chambersburg PA
CBHW052137010526
44113CB00036B/2305